TOP 10
HEAVYWEIGHT
BOXERS

Ron Knapp

**SPORTS
TOP 10**

 Enslow Publishers, Inc.

44 Fadem Road	PO Box 38
Box 699	Aldershot
Springfield, NJ 07081	Hants GU12 6BP
USA	UK

Library of Congress Cataloging-in-Publication Data

Knapp, Ron
    Top 10 heavyweight boxers / Ron Knapp.
      p. cm. — (Sports top 10)
    Includes bibliographical references (p.) and index.
    Summary: Profiles the lives and careers of Muhammed Ali, Jack Dempsey,
George Foreman, Joe Louis, Joe Frazier, Larry Holmes, Jack Johnson, Rocky
Marciano, John L. Sullivan, and Mike Tyson.
    ISBN 0-89490-806-5
    1. Boxers (Sports)—Biography—Juvenile literature. 2. Boxers (Sports)—
Rating of—Juvenile literature. [1. Boxers (Sports)] I. Title. II. Series.
GV1131.K53 1997
796.8'3'0922—dc21
[B]   96-52841
                                            CIP
                                            AC

Printed in the United States of America

10 9 8 7 6 5 4 3 2 1

Illustration Credits: Bauman Photography, Inc., pp. 35, 37; BETTMANN,
p. 43; CORBIS-BETTMANN, p. 41; Denver Public Library Western History
Department, pp. 26, 29; National Archives, p. 33; Reproduced from the
Collections of the Library of Congress, pp. 11, 39; REUTERS/CORBIS-
BETTMANN, p. 17; UPI/BETTMANN, pp. 6, 9, 21, 23, 45; UPI/CORBIS-
BETTMANN, pp. 13, 14, 19, 25, 30.

Cover Illustration: UPI/BETTMANN NEWSPHOTOS.

Interior Design: Richard Stalzer

CONTENTS

Introduction

BOXING CAN BE A BRUTAL sport. In games like basketball and football, competitors are penalized for trying to hurt their opponents. But the quickest way for a boxer to win is to hurt his opponent so badly that he cannot continue.

Fights in ancient Greece didn't end until the winning boxer had beaten his opponent to death. Two thousand years ago Roman fighters wore leather hand straps covered with metal.

But throughout history, efforts have been made to make boxing a safer sport. By the eighteenth century, fights were usually divided into rounds. Whenever a man was knocked down, the round ended. There was no rest period; the action was continuous until one fighter could no longer continue. An 1849 fight in Edenbridge, England, lasted 185 rounds and more than six hours. Boxers fought with their bare knuckles, and they were allowed to wrestle their opponents to the ground. The Queensberry Rules, introduced in 1866, required soft gloves and limited rounds to three minutes.

Today boxers have to pass physicals, and doctors are on duty at ringside. Professional title fights are now usually limited to just twelve rounds. When a man is knocked down, he is given ten seconds to get back up. Boxers are penalized for hitting below the belt. They have to wear mouthpieces.

Despite the rule changes, boxing is still a dangerous sport. The possibility of serious injury—or even death—is always there. Three-time heavyweight champion Muhammad Ali today suffers from symptoms similar to Parkinson's syndrome, probably caused by the punches he took to the head during his long career.

Few sporting events are as exciting as a fight. Sometimes a boxer puts on an awesome display of power that quickly dispatches an opponent. Other classic matches have been marked by determination and courage that kept boxers on their feet when they were exhausted.

Today, in the United States, most public attention is focused on the largest fighters, the heavyweights. Boxers who weigh 190 pounds or more compete in this division. Thousands of them participate in amateur bouts, and a few of them are good enough to become professionals. Heavyweight champions are among the highest-paid athletes in the world.

The men in this book earned their reputations by taking the heavyweight title and keeping it. Most of them relied more on strength than speed, but, despite their size, they all had to be able to move quickly around the ring. Just as important, they had to have the stamina—and the courage—to stand up against an avalanche of punches. Despite their differing styles and attitudes, these ten men were recognized by millions of fans as the toughest fighters on the planet.

CAREER STATISTICS

Boxer	Wins	Losses	Draws	KO
MUHAMMAD ALI	56	5	0	37
JACK DEMPSEY	60	6	8	50
GEORGE FOREMAN	76	4	0	68
JOE FRAZIER	32	4	1	27
LARRY HOLMES	65	6	0	42
JACK JOHNSON	68	10	10	40
JOE LOUIS	68	3	0	54
ROCKY MARCIANO	49	0	0	43
JOHN L. SULLIVAN	38	1	3	33
MIKE TYSON	45	2	0	39

KO= knock outs

MUHAMMAD ALI

Muhammad Ali during his championship bout with Floyd Patterson, in Las Vegas, Nevada. Ali retained the heavyweight title by knocking out Patterson in the twelfth round.

MUHAMMAD ALI

CASSIUS CLAY, AS MUHAMMAD ALI was known when he was a young man, probably never would have become a boxer if neighborhood bullies hadn't stolen his bicycle when he was twelve. A policeman in Louisville, Kentucky, convinced young Cassius to take up the sport so that he could defend himself if they tried it again.

Years later, the young champion was a talkative but likable young athlete. He was handsome and popular. Soon, it became obvious he wasn't like most other fighters. Clay liked to brag about his boxing skills. He predicted to reporters how long opponents would last in the ring against him. In 1964, he prepared to fight Sonny Liston for the heavyweight title. Clay called him "a big, ugly bear" and predicted he would knock him out in eight rounds.[1]

Clay's strategy against Liston was simple: "Float like a butterfly, sting like a bee."[2] The big man chased him around the ring, swinging powerfully but wildly, going for a quick knockout. Clay danced backward, and dodged punches by leaning way back. After a few rounds, Liston got tired and frustrated. Then Clay began "stinging" him with quick, sharp jabs. After six rounds, the big man gave up, and the "Louisville Lip" was champion.

Soon after, Clay announced that after many months of studying with the minister Malcolm X, he had become a follower of the Nation of Islam and would have a new name, Muhammad Ali.

In 1967, because of his new religion, Ali felt it would be wrong to fight in the Vietnam War. When he was drafted by the U.S. Army, he refused to join, and he was arrested. Soon various boxing commissions took away his title. Ali lost millions of dollars during the three years he was prevented from boxing.

Ali took his case to the United States Supreme Court. In 1971, just before winning his case, he was allowed to return to the ring. In "The Fight of the Century," the current champion, Joe Frazier, threw punch after punch as Ali spent much of the bout against the ropes. Ali expected his opponent to tire, but Joe just kept coming. In the fifteenth and final round, Frazier caught Ali with a left hook and dropped him to the canvas. Ali got up, but he lost a unanimous decision.

Three years later, Ali took a twelve-round decision from Frazier. His next fight, called the "Rumble in the Jungle," was in Kinshasa, Zaire, against George Foreman, the new champ. Ali absorbed punch after punch, usually on his arms as he guarded his face, but he didn't go down. By the seventh round, Foreman was tired. Then Ali left the ropes and went after the champion. In the eighth, Foreman collapsed to the canvas. Ali was once again champ!

In 1975, Ali and Frazier squared off in the Philippines for the "Thrilla in Manila." This time Ali tried to destroy his opponent in the early rounds, but Frazier refused to go down. It was a gruesome spectacle that didn't end until Frazier was unable to come out for the fifteenth.

During the two decades that he dominated heavyweight boxing, Ali was much more than just a fighter. His sense of humor, and his brave stands for his religion and against the Vietnam War, gradually won him the respect and affection of millions of people around the world. By 1996, he was a popular choice to light the Olympic flame in Atlanta.

While training for a fight, he said, "I can't lose, cause I'm fightin' for people all over the world. If I win, people all over the world's gonna win. If I lose, they all gonna lose."[3]

MUHAMMAD ALI

BORN: January 17, 1942; Louisville, Kentucky.

OLYMPIC CHAMPION: 1960 light heavyweight.

RING MAGAZINE FIGHTER OF THE YEAR: 1963, 1972, 1974, 1975, 1978.

CHAMPION: 1964–67, 1974–78, 1978–79.

OPPONENTS IN TITLE FIGHTS: Sonny Liston, Floyd Patterson, George Chuvalo, Henry Cooper, Brian London, Karl Mildenberger, Cleveland Williams, Ernie Terrell, Zora Folley, George Foreman, Chuck Wepner, Ron Lyle, Joe Bugner, Joe Frazier, Jean Pierre Coopman, Jimmy Young, Richard Dunn, Ken Norton, Alfredo Evangelista, Earnie Shavers, and Leon Spinks. He was stripped of his title in 1967, lost to Frazier in 1971, lost to Spinks in 1978, then retired as champion in 1979, after a rematch. Came out of retirement and lost to Larry Holmes in 1980.

Muhammad Ali delivers a bone-rattling punch to the head of Ken Norton. Many consider Muhammad Ali to be the best heavyweight boxer of all time.

JACK DEMPSEY

WHEN HE WAS A TEENAGER, Jack Dempsey worked as a lumberjack, a miner, and a fruit picker. He didn't mind the hard work, but he wanted to earn some real money. With just an eighth-grade education, he decided his best chance to get rich was to become a boxer.

Dempsey was strong, and he was determined to be a champion. He spent endless hours exercising and sparring. To make his skin tough, he soaked his hands, face, and neck in brine. To strengthen his jaw muscles, he chewed gum constantly.

In his early fights, he learned to crouch low to give his opponents a smaller, more protected target. From that position, it was also easy to unleash a devastating punch. Dempsey quickly gained a reputation as a hard puncher. As soon as the bell rang, he charged, trying to destroy his opponent as quickly as possible. His strategy was summed up by his trainer: "Pull up your socks, smack the big bum down and let's get this thing over with, kid."[1]

Dempsey wasn't a big man; he was just 6 feet tall and around 180 pounds. His size didn't stop him from knocking out bigger men, many of them in the first round earning him the nickname Jack the Giant-Killer. He was also called the Manassa Mauler, after his birthplace, Manassa, Colorado.

Dempsey met Jess Willard for the heavyweight title in 1919 at an outdoor arena in Toledo, Ohio. The temperature was 106 degrees. Willard was a huge man, bigger by six inches and seventy pounds. Dempsey had to stand on his toes so his punches could connect to the bigger man's head.

Early in the first round, Dempsey landed a crushing

JACK DEMPSEY

Known as "Jack the Giant-Killer," Jack Dempsey was able to dominate opponents much taller and heavier than himself.

blow to Willard's face. Suddenly the champ was sitting on the canvas looking up at the Giant-Killer. Seven times Dempsey decked him in the opening round.

The second round was more of the same—a bloody mess. By the third round, Willard's cheek was broken. When Willard couldn't answer the bell for the fourth, Jack Dempsey was the champion.

Gene Tunney was a completely different fighter. Unlike Dempsey, he didn't attempt to destroy his opponents; he tried to win by outsmarting them. In their 1926 title fight, he backed away from Dempsey's charges, avoiding his big punches while landing sharp jabs of his own. The strategy frustrated Dempsey and earned Tunney a ten-round decision.

Dempsey was determined to regain his title, and one year later, they met again. Tunney had the same fight plan, and, for the first six rounds, it worked.

In the seventh round Dempsey ignored his exhaustion and pain, and gathered all his remaining strength. He went after Tunney with everything he had left. Pow! A solid right connected. Then a left hook and a series of shots. Tunney was down!

The referee began counting, but had to stop when Dempsey failed to move away. Instead of going to a neutral corner, he just stood over his fallen opponent, too exhausted to move. The referee had to push him away before resuming the count. The delay gave Tunney time to regain his senses. By the time the ref yelled "nine," he was back on his feet.

In the eighth round, it was Dempsey who was knocked down. After ten rounds, Tunney was awarded a unanimous decision. Ever since then, boxing fans have argued about the long count. Was Dempsey cheated out of a victory? No way, said the Manassa Mauler. "The referee was not responsible; Tunney was not responsible. I should have been in the neutral corner."[2]

JACK DEMPSEY

BORN: June 24, 1895; Manassa, Colorado.

DIED: May 31, 1983; New York, New York.

CHAMPION: 1919–26.

OPPONENTS IN TITLE FIGHTS: Jess Willard, Billy Miske, Bill Brennan, Georges Carpentier, Tommy Gibbons, and Louis Firpo. He lost to Gene Tunney in 1926 and 1927.

On July 4, 1919, Jack Dempsey won the heavyweight title by knocking out Jess Willard in the fourth round. Dempsey held the title until 1926.

GEORGE FOREMAN

After leaving the sport of boxing in the late 1970s, George Foreman returned to the ring in the mid 1980s and became a fan favorite.

GEORGE FOREMAN

NANCY REE FOREMAN, GEORGE'S MOTHER, called him Monkey because "when he was a baby he just couldn't keep still, and he was so quick and strong."[1] By the time he was a teenager, Foreman had used his athletic skills to become an amateur boxing champion.

At the 1968 Olympics in Mexico City, he met Ionas Chepulis of the USSR, for the heavyweight gold medal. "Whenever Chepulis came forward, I stuck out a left jab," Foreman said. "He kept charging me and running into it."[2] That strategy prevented Chepulis from unloading his powerful right, allowing Foreman to pound him instead. Soon the referee stopped the fight, and Foreman was the Olympic champion.

As a professional, after a long string of victories, he met heavyweight champion Joe Frazier in 1973. Almost as soon as the fight started, Foreman blasted him with a thunderous uppercut. Down went Frazier! As soon as he got up, Foreman dropped him again with another uppercut.

Frazier was helpless. He had just enough strength to keep getting up. Foreman knocked him down five times, but he was still back on his feet. Foreman got mad. Why couldn't Frazier stay down? "All right," Foreman growled. "I'm going to kill him!"[3] The next time Frazier went down, the referee stopped the fight, and George Foreman was the new champion.

In 1974, Foreman destroyed Ken Norton in just two rounds, then screamed at Muhammad Ali, who was at ringside, "I'm going to kill you!"[4] He was earning a reputation as a vicious fighter. Foreman met Ali later that year at the "Rumble in the Jungle" in Zaire.

Foreman took off after Ali as soon as the bell sounded. For most of the fight, he had him backed into the ropes. "I fought a foolish fight by not letting him come to me more,"[5] Foreman recalled. Finally, Ali came off the ropes, landing punches that caught Foreman off balance and sent him to the canvas.

After six more bouts, Foreman retired from boxing to become a minister at a small church in Houston, Texas. For ten years, he devoted his time to preaching and running his church's youth camp. But, by 1987, the camp had run out of money and was in danger of closing. Foreman had an idea: "I know how to get money. I'm going to be heavyweight champ of the world. Again."[6]

When he met heavyweight champion Michael Moorer in 1994, Foreman was forty-five-years-old and weighed 250 pounds. Very few fans took him seriously, but most of them were cheering for him. No longer did he scowl or threaten to kill fighters he didn't like. For the first nine rounds, Moorer landed punch after punch while Foreman plodded around the ring, waiting for his chance.

All Moorer had to do was finish the fight, and the decision was his. Then, in the 10th round, Foreman got his chance. Moorer had slowed, and the gloves in front of his face were just a little too far apart. Foreman smashed his forehead with a punch that was so hard it made his hand ache. Moorer was staggered. After two more punches, he was flat on his back. As the referee counted out the fallen champion, Foreman knelt down in a corner and prayed. Once again, after twenty years, he was the champ.

"I'm not saying I'm great," he told reporters. "I'm nothing near great. But this, boxing, is me. It's what I do. Boxing was invented for me, and nobody else. . . . This is easy. I'm almost 50, but this is what I do. . . . What I am is a force of nature."[7]

GEORGE FOREMAN

BORN: January 10, 1949; Marshall, Texas.

OLYMPIC CHAMPION: 1968 super heavyweight.

RING MAGAZINE FIGHTER OF THE YEAR: 1973, 1976.

CHAMPION: 1973–74, 1994–95.

OPPONENTS IN TITLE FIGHTS: Joe Frazier, Jose Roman, Ken Norton, Michael Moorer, and Axel Schulz. He lost to Muhammad Ali in 1974. Lost to Evander Holyfield in 1991.

Lining up his next punch, George Foreman looks to connect on Michael Moorer. In this 1994 bout, Foreman knocked out Moorer in the 10th round to become the oldest person to ever win the heavyweight title at age forty-five.

Joe Frazier

JOE FRAZIER WAS A TOUGH chubby kid growing up in Beaufort, South Carolina. "I had my share of street fights . . . ," he said. "Nobody ever beat me and I just figured nobody could whip me."[1] After dropping out of school in the tenth grade, he moved north to Philadelphia, where he began working out at a gym to lose weight. That's where he learned to box.

In the 1964 Olympics, he broke his left hand in an early bout, but kept fighting and won the super heavyweight gold medal. He was an aggressive boxer, who hit hard with both hands and never stopped going after his opponents. "He's quick—surprisingly quick," said Jerry Quarry, who was knocked out by Frazier. "He's there all the time. He makes most guys panic."[2] Frazier said his style was simple: "I'm comin' out smokin'."[3] He earned the nickname Smokin' Joe.

In a 1970 fight for the heavyweight championship, three hard Frazier hooks to the mouth, abdomen, and chin stunned Jimmy Ellis. Another left hook to the head and he hit the canvas. Ellis got up at the count of nine, but quickly Frazier belted him with a pair of hooks before taking a soft shot to the jaw. A hard right to the body, and Ellis was finished. He couldn't answer the bell for the sixth round.

Smokin' Joe had the title, but to earn the respect of the boxing world he had to beat Muhammad Ali. "If Joe Frazier whups me, I'm gonna get down on my knees right in the ring. . . . ," Ali said, "and I'll crawl across and say, 'You are the greatest.'"[4] The bout, called "The Fight of the Century," on March 8, 1971, was one of the most anticipated sporting events in history. More than 300 million people around the world watched on closed-circuit television.

JOE FRAZIER

At the 1964 Olympic Games in Tokyo, Japan, Joe Frazier defeated German Hans Huber to win the gold medal in the Super Heavyweight division.

In the opening rounds, Ali teased Frazier by tapping him playfully on the head instead of punching back. When Frazier belted him, he turned to the crowd and smiled, pretending that he didn't hurt. The fight was even until the 10th round when Frazier clobbered Ali's head with a left hook, then drove two more and a right into his body. By then, Ali was done teasing and smiling; he could barely stay on his feet.

In the 15th and last round, Ali charged, hoping for a knockdown.[5] Instead, Frazier dropped him briefly with a massive left hook. When Frazier was awarded a unanimous decision, Ali told him, "You the champ."[6]

After easily knocking out two opponents, Frazier didn't make it through two rounds against George Foreman in 1973. He was knocked down six times before the fight was stopped. Two years later, he tried to regain the title when he again met Ali, who had defeated Foreman. It was the "Thrilla in Manila," one of the most memorable fights of all time.

Late in the sixth round, Frazier went to work with his left hook. Two vicious blows exploded on Ali's jaw. The champ wobbled but didn't fall. Frazier landed punch after punch, but so did Ali. Late in the fight, Frazier ran out of steam and Ali began to target his head. The skin swelled around his eyes until he could barely see, but he refused to quit. Just before the 15th round, his manager, Eddie Futch, said he was going to stop the fight. "No, no, Eddie, ya can't do that to me," Frazier begged. He got up, but Futch pushed him back. "Sit down, son. It's all over. No one will ever forget what you did here."[7]

Back at the start of the seventh round, Ali had paid Frazier a rare compliment: "Old Joe Frazier, why I thought you were washed up." Smokin' Joe answered, "Somebody told you all wrong, pretty boy."[8]

JOE FRAZIER

BORN: January 12, 1944; Beaufort, South Carolina.

OLYMPIC CHAMPION: 1964 super heavyweight.

RING MAGAZINE FIGHTER OF THE YEAR: 1967, 1970, 1971.

CHAMPION: 1970–73.

OPPONENTS IN TITLE FIGHTS: Buster Mathis, Manuel Ramos, Oscar
Bonavena, Dave Zyglewicz, Jerry Quarry, Jimmy Ellis, Bob
Foster, Muhammad Ali, Terry Daniels, Ron Stander. He lost
to George Foreman in 1973 and to Muhammad Ali in 1975.

Unleashing a barrage of punches, Joe Frazier pounds on Buster
Mathis. Frazier beat Mathis to win the heavyweight championship
on March 4, 1968.

LARRY HOLMES

WITH TWELVE CHILDREN, THE HOLMES family couldn't afford to buy new shoes. "I remember us getting shoes at rummage sales in Georgia," said Larry Holmes.[1] When he was seven, his family moved to Easton, Pennsylvania, where his father hoped to find work. Larry got into trouble at school and with the police. "He wasn't a bad boy," his mother said, "but out on the streets he was mean. He didn't take nothing from nobody."[2]

He learned to box at a youth center in Easton. Holmes was quick; his hands and legs always seemed to be moving. His best punches were a fast jab and a powerful hook.

He was also tough. In a fight against Roy Williams, he broke his right thumb, but he kept swinging and won the decision. Then on June 10, 1978, he faced the heavyweight champion, Ken Norton. In the early rounds, Holmes out-boxed his opponent, but then in the sixth round, the champ clobbered his left shoulder. The blow was hard enough to tear a muscle. The pain made him wince. It hurt so much that his left arm was almost useless.

Holmes had nine rounds left and only one good hand. He managed to defend himself, but Norton began winning round after round. Going into the 15th and final round, Holmes knew it was going to come down to a close decision. Fighting virtually one-handed, he bravely went after Norton, popping him repeatedly with his strong right hand. The judges gave him the decision and the title.

Holmes's next big fight was one he didn't want. In 1980, Muhammad Ali came out of retirement to again go after the championship. "When I beat him," Holmes predicted,

LARRY HOLMES

Larry Holmes celebrates his knockout of challenger David Bey by holding up his International Boxing Federation Championship belt.

"they're gonna say he was an old man, and if I lose they're gonna say I was never nothing."[3]

Ali slimmed down and trained hard for the fight, but in the first round he couldn't stay away from Holmes's jabs. After being blasted in the head, Ali knew he was finished, but he wouldn't quit. He spent much of the rest of the fight leaning on the ropes. After ten rounds of punishment, Ali could fight no more.

The next year, Holmes went up against Leon Spinks, another former champ. When he heard a bell in the second round, Holmes dropped his hands and quit fighting. However, the bell was a mistake, and there were still twenty-five seconds left in the round. Spinks didn't stop; he kept punching. Holmes was furious. Why would Spinks hit a man who wasn't even defending himself?

Larry Holmes was determined to punish Spinks. When the third round started, he took off after the challenger, crashing a left hook into his abdomen. Before Spinks could recover, he knocked him back with a right to the jaw. Then he chased him into a corner and dropped him with three powerful blows. Spinks bravely got up at the count of nine, but he could barely stand. As Holmes closed in for the kill, the referee stopped the fight.

In 1982, Holmes finished off Gerry Cooney in a battle that earned each of them $10 million, the biggest payday up to that point in athletic history. His jabs kept Cooney from using his powerful left hook. Larry knocked him down in the second round and dominated the rest of the fight. In the 13th round, Cooney had had enough. When he staggered into the ropes, the fight was stopped.

Over twelve years, Holmes won forty-eight straight bouts. Eventually almost everybody believed the boast he had made while training for the Ali fight: "I'm the baddest . . . heavyweight in the world today."[4]

LARRY HOLMES

BORN: November 3, 1949; Cuthbert, Georgia.

RING MAGAZINE FIGHTER OF THE YEAR: 1982.

CHAMPION: 1980–85.

OPPONENTS IN TITLE FIGHTS: Ken Norton, Alfredo Evangelista, Osvaldo Ocasio, Mike Weaver, Earnie Sheavers, Lorenzo Zanon, Leroy Jones, Scott LeDoux, Muhammad Ali, Trevor Berbick, Leon Spinks, Renaldo Snipes, Gerry Cooney, Tex Cobb, Lucien Rodriguez, Tim Witherspoon, Scott Frank, Marvis Frazier, James Bonecrusher Smith, David Bey, and Carl Williams. He lost to Michael Spinks in 1985, and 1986. Lost to Mike Tyson in 1988. Lost to Evander Holyfield in 1992. Lost to Oliver McCall in 1995.

Stunning his adversary, Larry Holmes lands a clear shot on the face of Michael Spinks. In 1985, Spinks ended Holmes's seven-year-run as a heavyweight champion.

JACK JOHNSON

Showing off his championship form, Jack Johnson trains for his next fight. Johnson held the heavyweight championship for over six years.

JACK JOHNSON

JACK JOHNSON'S FIRST FIGHTS WERE against other African Americans in sideshow exhibitions called Battles Royal. The bouts weren't serious boxing; sometimes the fighters were even blindfolded. African-American athletes received very little respect in any sport. It would be almost half a century before Jackie Robinson became the first black major league baseball player.

Johnson, however, wasn't interested in waiting, and he wasn't satisfied with being an entertainer for white audiences. He wanted to be a serious professional prizefighter. Despite the widespread prejudice against black Americans, he challenged—and beat—many white fighters.

Johnson became known as a powerful defensive fighter who stood straight up in the ring and rarely allowed his opponents to get a good shot at him. He frustrated them by getting close enough to tangle their arms in his. Then he would unleash his own power, usually enough to end the fight. In the ring, he was an imposing sight with his shaved head and massive physique.

James L. Jeffries, heavyweight champ from 1899 to 1905, refused to fight Johnson because he was African American. It wasn't until 1908 that Johnson got a shot at the title when Tommy Burns, the new champ, agreed to fight. The bout was a joke. Johnson pointed to the right side of his abdomen and said, "Hit here, Tommy." Burns socked him there, and Johnson smiled. "Now here, Tommy." Burns again followed directions, bringing another smile.[1] Finally, in the 14th round, Johnson dropped Burns and became the first African-American heavyweight champion.

Many whites were outraged; they hated the idea of a black man's being recognized as the world's best boxer. Promoters began looking for "a great white hope" to defeat Johnson. Jeffries came out of retirement to "teach the black champ a lesson." Their July 4, 1910, match-up in Reno, Nevada, was viewed as a battle of the races. Across the country, thousands gathered outside newspaper offices to hear the results of each round. As Johnson stepped into the ring, the crowd greeted him with a racist song.[2]

For fourteen rounds, Johnson taunted Jeffries, daring him to punch, then laughing when the punches had no effect. Along the way, he kept pounding on Jeffries's head, finally causing his right eye to swell shut. Then, in the 15th round, the fight was stopped.

The victory earned Johnson little respect from white America. A typical headline read, "JEFFRIES MASTERED BY GRINNING, JEERING NEGRO."[3] Riots broke out in several cities as whites retaliated for the defeat by attacking blacks. Many communities outlawed the showing of films of his fights.

Johnson never tried to endear himself to white fans. He continued to infuriate his opponents by ridiculing them. One of his tricks was to back a man into a corner, pinning down his arms. "Then he would smile sweetly and kiss them on the cheek. Man, this would make these fighters so mad they would forget about boxing and come out swinging wild."[4]

Very few athletes in American history have ever had as much fun or been as intensely hated as Jack Johnson. A newspaper editor wrote, "Johnson fought a great fight. . . . It must be remembered, too, that it was the fight of one lone black man against the world."[5]

JACK JOHNSON

BORN: March 31, 1878; Galveston, Texas.

DIED: June 10, 1946; Raleigh, North Carolina.

CHAMPION: 1908–15.

OPPONENTS IN TITLE FIGHTS: Tommy Burns, Victor McLaglen, Philadelphia Jack O'Brien, Tony Ross, Al Kaufman, Stanley Ketchel, James L. Jeffries, Jim Flynn, Jim Johnson, and Frank Moran. He lost to Jess Willard in 1915.

Extremely confident, Jack Johnson seems to be enjoying his meeting with Tommy Burns. Johnson became the first African American to win the heavyweight championship when he knocked out Burns in the 14th round.

JOE LOUIS

Joe Louis shows off the stare he used to intimidate his opponents. Louis became heavyweight champion in 1937, after knocking out James J. Braddock.

JOE LOUIS, "THE BROWN BOMBER," was the first African-American athlete to gain the admiration of all Americans. He was world famous when the major-league sports of baseball, football, and basketball were still closed to African Americans.

When Louis fought Max Schmeling for the first time in 1936, most Americans felt that Louis stood for the things that were right with their country: freedom, decency, and determination. Schmeling, on the other hand, was from Germany, then ruled by Adolf Hitler and the Nazis. It became more than a prizefight; it was a battle between two very different systems. African Americans were especially interested in the outcome. For them, Louis was a symbol of what African Americans could do if they weren't held back by unfair laws.

The fight was even until the fourth round, when Schmeling stunned Louis with a vicious right cross to the face, then a right uppercut and a left cross. Louis tried to protect his head, but he was too dazed to return a punch. When the German landed another right to his chin, Louis hit the canvas—the first time in his professional career that he had ever been knocked down. He quickly jumped back up, but he got weaker and weaker as the fight dragged on. Schmeling finished him off with a barrage of punches in the twelfth round.

The loss to Schmeling wouldn't deter Louis from reaching his goal. On June 22, 1937, a hot night in Chicago, he met the champion Jim Braddock at Comiskey Park.

In the first round, Louis again was knocked down, this time by a flurry of punches. When he got up, his head was still clear and he knew what he had to do. For the next seven rounds, he went after the champion, chasing him around the ring, trading punches. By the eighth, Braddock was exhausted. His punches either missed or weren't strong enough to hurt. Finally, Louis put him away with a hard right. Braddock landed on his face, out cold.

Black Americans "went wildly happy with the greatest celebration of race pride our generation had ever known," wrote Malcolm X. "Every Negro boy old enough to walk wanted to be the next Brown Bomber."[1]

The rematch with Max Schmeling came exactly one year later in New York City. More than seventy thousand fans crowded into Yankee Stadium to see if Louis could redeem himself against the German. The Bomber was ready to avenge his embarrassing defeat. At the sound of the bell, he charged Schmeling, attacking his head with a pair of jabs, then two lefts, a hook, and an uppercut. By then, Schmeling was backed into the ropes. Louis faked a shot with his right, then clobbered him in the head with a left hook. The German was in trouble before he had even thrown a punch.

Louis kept up the pressure. Schmeling threw only two punches; one was blocked, the other missed. He could do nothing but cover up and move back.

Then Louis popped him in the jaw, dropping him for a three-count. When Schmeling got up, a series of quick punches sent him back down again. After a count of two, he got up, only to be greeted by a pair of hooks and a right to the jaw that laid him out for good. The fight had taken only two minutes and four seconds.

A reporter wrote, "He's the greatest fighter I ever saw, or ever expect to see. Somebody'll beat him. But nobody will ever beat the Joe Louis you saw last night. Not a Joe Louis who is young, well-trained—and mad."[2]

JOE LOUIS

BORN: May 13, 1914; Lafayette, Alabama.

DIED: April 12, 1981; Las Vagas, Nevada.

RING MAGAZINE FIGHTER OF THE YEAR: 1936, 1938, 1939, 1941.

CHAMPION: 1937–49.

OPPONENTS IN TITLE FIGHTS: James J. Braddock, Tommy Farr, Nathan Mann, Harry Thomas, Max Schmeling, John Henry Lewis, Jack Roper, Tony Galento, Bob Pastor, Arturo Godoy (2), Johnny Paycheck, Al McCoy, Red Burman, Gus Dorazio, Abe Simon (2), Tony Musto, Buddy Baer (2), Billy Conn (2), Lou Nova, Tami Mauriello, and Jersey Joe Walcott (2) He retired as champion in 1949, then lost to Ezzard Charles in 1950.

1937	1948	
23	AGE	34
	WEIGHT	
197¼		214 LBS.
	NECK	
16½ IN.		17 IN.
	CHEST NORMAL	
41 IN.		42 IN.
	CHEST EXPANDED	
44 IN.		45 IN.
	BICEPS	
14 IN.		15 IN.
	WAIST	
34 IN.		36½ IN.
	THIGH	
21 IN.		22½ IN.

JOE LOUIS

Joe Louis held the heavyweight title from 1937 to 1949. He was named *Ring* magazine's Fighter of the Year four times, 1936, 1938–39, and 1941.

ROCKY MARCIANO

YOUNG ROCKY MARCIANO HAD DREAMS of becoming a professional football or baseball player. After quitting high school, he had no chance to play football in college, a necessary stepping-stone to the pros. When he realized he was too slow to be a baseball star, he turned to boxing.

Rocky really wasn't built to be a heavyweight. He was short (5 feet 10½ inches) and light (185 pounds). His arms were stubby; when he stretched them out, they only measured 68 inches from fingertip to fingertip. Jack Dempsey measured 77 inches, Joe Louis 76, and Muhammad Ali 82.[1] His short arms kept him from jabbing at his opponents from a distance. He had to get in close and overwhelm them with his power.

One of Marciano's earliest pro fights almost ended in tragedy. After five brutal rounds, Carmine Vingo was too tired to hold his gloves up for protection, so Rocky attacked. Soon blood was pouring from Vingo's nostrils. A quick left hook knocked him backward on his head, and the referee ended the fight. Vingo couldn't get up; soon he lapsed into a coma. Marciano rushed to the hospital to be with Vingo's family. The injury made him think about his sport. "He could have done this to me. . . ." he said. "I could have been in his shoes."[2] After a few days, Vingo came out of his coma. He had survived the fight. Marciano returned to his quest for the heavyweight title.

In 1951, a solid Marciano hook dropped former champion Joe Louis in the eighth round. "That punch made all my dreams come true," Marciano said. "But it was the saddest punch of my life. How else could I feel seeing . . . one

Going at him full force, Rocky Marciano connects with a blow to the head of Jersey Joe Walcott.

of the finest sportsmen that ever lived lying there on the canvas?"[3]

A year later, Jersey Joe Walcott, the reigning champion, knocked him down in the first round with a left hook. Marciano jumped up after a two-count, but spent the next dozen rounds taking a vicious beating. Walcott was far ahead on points in the thirteenth round when Marciano charged. "Walcott is back to the ropes," the radio announcer said. "Takes a right to the jaw! Walcott is down on his stomach and they're counting over him! . . . He is still out cold. It's a knockout and we have a new heavyweight champion of the world!"[4]

In 1955, Marciano collided with Archie Moore, the light heavyweight champion who wanted to pick up another title. Marciano was dropped by a shot to the chin in the second, but after that, the fight was fairly even as the men traded punches. Finally Marciano's right glove smashed into Moore's head. He was flat on his back at the count of six when he was saved by the bell. After he struggled to his feet, a doctor asked him if he wanted to continue. "I, too, am a champion," Moore said proudly. "And I'll go down fighting."[5]

When the bell rang again, Marciano crowded Moore into the ropes, where he finished him with a barrage of punches. It was Marciano's last fight. He was the only man ever to retire undefeated as the heavyweight champ.

"Nature gave Rocky everything he needs as a champion," said his manager, Al Weill. "He has unusual strength and stamina, a terrific punch and plenty of guts. No one ever trained harder or took better care of himself."[6]

ROCKY MARCIANO

BORN: September 1, 1923; Brocton, Massachusetts.

DIED: August 31, 1969; near Newton, Iowa.

RING MAGAZINE FIGHTER OF THE YEAR: 1952, 1954, 1955.

CHAMPION: 1952–56.

OPPONENTS IN TITLE FIGHTS: Jersey Joe Walcott (2), Roland LaStarza, Ezzard Charles (2), Don Cockell, Archie Moore. He retired as champion in 1956.

Landing a clean right hand, Marciano puts the hurt on Roland LaStarza. In 1953, Marciano knocked out LaStarza in the 11th round of their championship fight to retain the heavyweight title.

JOHN L. SULLIVAN

NOBODY IN BOSTON WAS AS strong as young John L. Sullivan. When he was a teenager, he showed off by lifting barrels of nails over his head. When a horsecar tipped off the tracks, Sullivan set it back in place with his bare hands.

Sullivan's parents wanted him to be a priest. After quitting Boston College, he decided to be a plumber instead. That job didn't last long; Sullivan got into a fight with his boss and broke his jaw.

He was at a variety show in 1877 when a boxer named Tom Scannell dared anybody in the audience to fight him. Sullivan had never boxed before, but he stepped onto the stage, took off his coat, and put on a pair of gloves. When he held out a glove to shake hands, Scannell laughed and punched him in the head. Sullivan went berserk. He charged Scannell, landing a punch that sent him flying off the stage into a piano. That quick fight convinced Sullivan that he could make a living as a boxer. Many of the most successful boxers then were, like him, Irish Americans.

Four years later, he fought Paddy Ryan for the heavyweight championship. Almost as soon as the bout started, Sullivan decked the champ with a mighty right to the chin. "I thought a telegraph pole had been shoved against me sideways," Ryan said.[1]

The champion got up, but he never had a chance. Ryan collapsed after just eleven minutes and couldn't get back up.

Sullivan's most memorable battle was in 1889 against Jake Kilrain. It was the last great bare-knuckle championship fight. Sitting under the blazing Richburg, Mississippi, sun, the crowd went wild as soon as Sullivan

John L. Sullivan displays his fighting stance. Though his parents wanted him to become a priest, Sullivan decided to fight for a living.

JOHN L. SULLIVAN

appeared and began flexing his back muscles. Kilrain, however, didn't bother flexing; he grabbed Sullivan by the neck and tossed him over his hip. After Sullivan pulled the same move on him, the boxers began trading punches.

Then Kilrain changed his strategy. Instead of punching Sullivan, he kept backpedaling. When he was in danger of being hit, he fell to the ground, stopping the action. When he couldn't catch Kilrain, Sullivan got frustrated—and tired. In the 45th round, he started to vomit.

In the 68th round, Sullivan finally caught him. As the challenger was starting to go down again, the champion's fist exploded under his chin, raising him up off the grass. After that, Kilrain was in a daze. He finally had to quit after the 75th. The incredible battle had lasted two hours and fifteen minutes.

When Sullivan faced Gentleman Jim Corbett in 1892, he wore the new large padded gloves for the first time. In the third round, Corbett's left exploded in Sullivan's face. Blood spewed from his broken nose, drenching his face and chest. Then Corbett went after his midsection. Sullivan bent over in pain, but the challenger couldn't finish him off.

By the 14th round, Sullivan could no longer raise his arms high enough to protect his face. In the 21st round, Gentleman Jim landed a hard right to the jaw that dropped Sullivan to his knees. Sullivan struggled to his feet. Two more punches, and it was all over.

A few moments later, the Champion of Champions grabbed the ring post and pulled himself to his feet. When he began to speak the crowd fell silent. "All I have to say is that I came into the ring once too often—and if I had to get licked I'm glad I was licked by an American. I remain your warm and personal friend, John L. Sullivan."[2]

John L. Sullivan

BORN: October 15, 1858; Roxbury, Massachusetts.

DIED: February 2, 1918; Abington, Massachusetts.

CHAMPION: 1885–92.

OPPONENTS IN TITLE FIGHTS: Paddy Ryan, Charley Mitchell, Jake Kilrain. He lost to Gentleman Jim Corbett in 1892.

Sullivan took part in the last bare-knuckle championship fight, in which he defeated Jake Kilrain. In 1892, heavyweight championship fights began to follow the Queensberry Rules which required boxers to wear gloves.

MIKE TYSON

WHEN HE WAS A LITTLE boy growing up in Brooklyn, New York, Mike Tyson was very shy—and very scared of the neighborhood bullies. "They used to take my sneakers, my clothes, my money," he said. "Beat me up and smack me around."[1]

Tyson's hobby was raising and flying pigeons. One day one of the bullies stole a pigeon from him and broke its neck. In an instant, Tyson forgot about being shy and being scared. He tore into the bully, pounding him with his fists. It was the first time he ever fought, and it felt good.[2]

By the time he was thirteen years old, he was 5 feet 8 inches tall and weighed 210 pounds. Even adults were afraid of him. When his mother and teachers couldn't control him, he was sent to a reform school.

A counselor at the school offered to teach him to box if Tyson would work hard at his classes and behave himself. The boy kept his part of the deal and soon he had a reputation as one of the toughest young boxers in the country. He moved into the home of Cus D'Amato, a veteran trainer who began training him for a professional career.

Tyson's style was to keep his chin down and his gloves up. D'Amato trained him to chase his opponents while bobbing and weaving to keep them from hitting him. By then he was 5 feet 11 inches and 215 pounds. He was smaller than most of his opponents, but that didn't stop him from being an aggressive, powerful puncher. His explosive shots earned him nicknames like "Iron Mike" and "Kid Dynamite."[3] He was tough and mean in the ring; some of his opponents said he fought dirty. They complained about

MIKE TYSON

Mike Tyson looks on after knocking down James "Buster" Douglas in their 1990 championship fight.

the way he used his elbows when he was fighting at close range.

When Tyson was ready to fight other top heavyweights, the championship was split between three fighters, each backed by a different group. To become the undefeated champion, he had to beat all three of them. In the second round, he dropped Trevor Berbick with a left hook that bounced off the top of his head. When he whipped James "Bonecrusher" Smith and Tony Tucker in unanimous decisions, the undisputed title was his in 1987.

In a fourth-round clinch, Tyson knocked Larry Holmes to the canvas. When he got up, two lefts and a right to the head sent him back down. When that didn't stop him, an awesome right connected with his jaw, ending the fight. "I still don't like you," Holmes told Iron Mike, "but you can fight."[4]

After cracking Michael Spinks hard in the face with his elbow, Tyson knocked him down with a monstrous left uppercut and a powerful right to the ribs, then a blistering short right to the jaw and another knockdown. Spinks couldn't struggle back to his feet, and Tyson had a first-round knockout.

The champ looked unstoppable until Buster Douglas shocked him with a tenth-round knockout in 1990. Then, as Tyson struggled to regain his crown, he was arrested and convicted on rape charges. He spent three years in prison, then returned to the ring by demolishing Peter McNeeley in just eighty-nine seconds.

Tyson remains a fearsome boxer. "There is no fighter like me," he said confidently when he was champ. "I can beat any man in the world."[5]

MIKE TYSON

BORN: June 30, 1966; Brooklyn, New York.

RING MAGAZINE FIGHTER OF THE YEAR: 1986, 1988.

CHAMPION: 1987–90, 1996.

OPPONENTS IN TITLE FIGHTS: Trevor Birbeck, Bonecrusher Smith, Pinklon Thomas, Tony Tucker, Tyrell Biggs, Larry Holmes, Tony Tubbs, Michael Spinks, Frank Bruno (2), Carl Williams, Bruce Seldon. He lost to Buster Douglas in 1990, and Evander Holyfield in 1996.

With extreme power, Mike Tyson blasts Mitch Green with a shot to the face. Tyson regained a portion of the heavyweight title by knocking out Frank Bruno in 1996.

CHAPTER NOTES

Muhammad Ali

1. Muhammad Ali with Richard Durham, *The Greatest: My Own Story* (New York: Random House, 1975), p. 112.
2. Editors of Salem Press, *Great Athletes* (Pasadena, Calif.: Salem Press, 1992), p. 31.
3. Budd Schulberg, *Loser and Still Champion: Muhammad Ali* (Garden City, N.Y.: Doubleday & Company, Inc., 1971), p. 98.

Jack Dempsey

1. Jack Dempsey with Barbara Piattelli, *Dempsey* (New York: Harper & Row, 1977), p. 201.
2. Anna Rothe, ed., *Current Biography* (New York: H. W. Wilson Company, 1945), p. 146.

George Foreman

1. Charles Moritz, ed., *Current Biography* (New York: H. W. Wilson Company, 1974), p. 120.
2. George Foreman and Joe Engel, *By George* (New York: Villard Books, 1996), p. 59.
3. Ibid., p. 89.
4. Ibid., p. 101.
5. Ibid., p. 115.
6. Ibid., p. 225.
7. Richard Hoffer, "KO'd," *Sports Illustrated,* vol. 81, no. 20, November 14, 1994, p. 22.

Joe Frazier

1. Charles Moritz, ed., *Current Biography Yearbook* (New York: H. W. Wilson Company, 1971), p. 143.
2. John D. McCallum, *The World Heavyweight Boxing Championship* (Radnor, Pa.: Chilton Book Company, 1974), p. 343.
3. Ibid.
4. Ibid., p. 349.
5. Ibid., p. 351.
6. Muhammad Ali with Richard Durham, *The Greatest: My Own Story* (New York: Random House, 1975), p. 355.
7. Mark Kram, "Lawdy, Lawdy, He's Great," *Sports Illustrated,* vol. 81, no. 14, October 3, 1994, p. 34.
8. Ibid.

Larry Holmes

1. Jerry Izenberg, "An Angry Man in Search of Ali," *Sport,* vol. 71, no. 1, July 1980, p. 43.
2. Jerry Izenberg, *Lincoln Library of Sports Champions* (Columbus, Ohio: Frontier Press Company, 1985), vol. 8, p. 78.

3. Greg Walter, "Once Ali's Sparring Mate, Champ Larry Holmes Says Now He's 'The World's Baddest Heavyweight,'" *People,* vol. 14, no. 13, September 29, 1980, p. 89.

4. Ibid., p. 88.

Jack Johnson

1. John D. McCallum, *The World Heavyweight Boxing Championship* (Radnor, Pa.: Chilton Book Company, 1974), p. 62.

2. Al-Tony Gilmore, *The National Impact of Jack Johnson* (Port Washington, N.Y.: Kennikat Press, 1975), p. 42.

3. Ibid.

4. Ibid., p. 20.

5. Ibid., p. 140.

Joe Louis

1. Malcolm X with Alex Haley, *The Autobiography of Malcolm X* (New York: Ballantine Books, 1965), p. 23.

2. Chris Mead, *Champion: Joe Louis, Black Hero in White America* (New York: Charles Scribner's Sons, 1985), p. 56.

Rocky Marciano

1. John D. McCallum, *The World Heavyweight Boxing Championship* (Radnor, Pa.: Chilton Book Company, 1974), pp. 248–249.

2. Everett M. Skehan, *Rocky Marciano: Biography of a First Son* (Boston: Houghton Mifflin Company, 1977), p. 135.

3. Anna Rothe, ed., *Current Biography* (New York: H.W. Wilson Company, 1952), p. 404.

4. Don Dunphy, *Don Dunphy at Ringside* (New York: Henry Holt and Company, 1988), pp. 86–87.

5. Ibid., p. 243.

6. McCallum, p. 257.

John L. Sullivan

1. Nat Fleischer, *John L. Sullivan: Champion of Champions* (New York: G. P. Putnam's Sons, 1951), p. 49.

2. Fleischer, p. 49.

Mike Tyson

1. Charles Moritz, ed., *Current Biography Yearbook* (New York: H. W. Wilson Company, 1988), p. 579.

2. Peter Heller, *Bad Intentions: The Mike Tyson Story* (New York: New American Library, 1989), pp. 8–9.

3. Peter Heller, *Great Athletes* (Pasadena, Calif.: Salem Press, 1992), p. 2,599.

4. Reg Gutteride, *The Big Punchers* (London: Stanley Paul & Co., Ltd., 1989), p. 187.

5. Heller, p. 270.

INDEX

A
Ali, Muhammad (Cassius Clay), 4, 5, 6–9, 15–16, 18, 20, 22, 24, 34

B
Battles Royal, 27
Berbick, Trevor, 44
Boston College, 38
Braddock, Jim, 31–32
Burns, Tommy, 27

C
Chepulis, Ionas, 15
Cooney, Gerry, 24
Corbett, Gentleman Jim, 40

D
D'Amato, Cus, 42
Dempsey, Jack, 5, 10–13, 34
Douglas, Buster, 44

E
Ellis, Jimmy, 18

F
Foreman, George, 5, 14–17, 20
Foreman, Nancy Ree, 15
Frazier, Joe, 5, 8, 15, 18–21
Futch, Eddie, 20

H
Hitler, Adolf, 31
Holmes, Larry, 5, 22–25, 44

J
Jeffries, James L., 27, 28
Johnson, Jack, 5, 26–29

K
Kilrain, Jake, 38, 40

L
Liston, Sonny, 7
Louis, Joe, 5, 30–33, 34, 36

M
Malcolm X, 7, 32
Marciano, Rocky, 5, 34–37
Moore, Archie, 36
Moorer, Michael, 16

N
Nation of Islam, 7
Nazis, 31
Norton, Ken, 15, 22

O
Olympics (1964), 18
Olympics (1968), 15
Olympics (1996), 8

Q
Quarry, Jerry, 18
Queensberry Rules, 4

R
Robinson, Jackie, 27
Ryan, Paddy, 38

S
Scannell, Tom, 48
Schmeling, Max, 31, 32
Smith, James "Bonecrusher," 44
Spinks, Leon, 24
Spinks, Michael, 44
Sullivan, John L., 5, 38–41

T
Tucker, Tony, 44
Tunney, Gene, 12
Tyson, Mike, 5, 42–45

V
Vietnam War, 7
Vingo, Carmine, 34

W
Walcott, Jersey Joe, 36
Weill, Al, 36
Willard, Jess, 10